THE
Seven Wonders
OF THE ANCIENT WORLD

By Shirley Jordan

MOMENTS IN HISTORY

Perfection Learning®

About the Author

Shirley Jordan is a retired elementary school teacher and principal. For eight years, she was a lecturer in the teacher-training program at California State University, Fullerton, California.

Shirley loves to travel—with a preference for sites important to U.S. history. She has had more than 50 travel articles published in recent years. It was through her travels that she became interested in "moments in history," those ironic and little-known stories that make one exclaim, "I didn't know that!" Such stories are woven throughout her books.

Designer: Emily J. Greazel

Image Credits: © ARGOSY Illustration: pp. 11, 21, 27 (top), 34; © Dan Hatala: pp. 13, 23, 27 (bottom), 35, 42–43, 47, 55; © Archivo Iconografico, S.A./CORBIS: p. 32; © Gianni Dagli Orti/CORBIS: p. 25; © Art Resource: p. 43; © North Wind Picture Archives: pp. 20, 29, 48, 52–53

Art Today (some images copyright www.arttoday.com): pp. 7, 19, 37, 38, 46, 51, 57, 59, 60, 62; Corel Professional Photos: cover, pp. 9, 15, 16, 45, 50

For information, contact
Perfection Learning® Corporation,
1000 North Second Avenue,
P.O. Box 500, Logan, Iowa 51546-0500.
Tel: 1-800-831-4190 • Fax: 1-800-543-2745
perfectionlearning.com

1 2 3 4 5 6 PP 08 07 06 05 04 03

Paperback ISBN 0-7891-5918-x
Cover Craft® ISBN 0-7569-1188-5

TABLE OF CONTENTS

A TIMELINE OF IMPORTANT EVENTS

(Dates in italics are approximate.)

B.C.

2550	The Pharaoh Khufu orders a giant **tomb** built for his burial place.
776	The first official Olympic Games are held.
605–562	Nebuchadnezzar II rules Babylon and builds the Hanging Gardens.
550	The Temple of Artemis is built at Ephesus.
539	The Persian conqueror Cyrus leads an army against Babylon.
450	The **architect** Libon is hired to build a temple to Zeus.
435	The artist Phidias begins the Statue of Zeus at Olympia.
356	Herostratus sets fire to the Temple of Artemis.
350	The tomb of King Mausolus is completed at Halicarnassus.
332	Alexander the Great founds the city of Alexandria.
305–293	The Colossus of Rhodes is constructed.
300–280	The Lighthouse at Alexandria is built.

| 226 | An earthquake topples the Colossus of Rhodes. |
| 130 | Antipater of Sidon lists the Seven Wonders of the Ancient World. |

262	The Temple of Artemis is damaged by earthquakes and invaders.
391	The Romans end the Olympic Games.
426	The Temple of Zeus at Olympia is destroyed.
462	The Statue of Zeus is destroyed by fire at Constantinople.
654	Broken sections of the Colossus of Rhodes are carried away and sold for scrap metal.
1250	An earthquake topples the Mausoleum at Halicarnassus.
1324	The Lighthouse at Alexandria is destroyed by an earthquake.

CHAPTER 1

Who Chose the Seven Wonders?

More than 2000 years ago, writers who lived near the Mediterranean Sea began to keep records. One of those writers was Antipater of Sidon. Antipater was Greek, and he was known for his fine poetry.

Like many poets of his time, Antipater liked to travel. He went from place to place to see the excellent buildings and statues all around the Mediterranean. Such places of beauty gave him ideas for his writing.

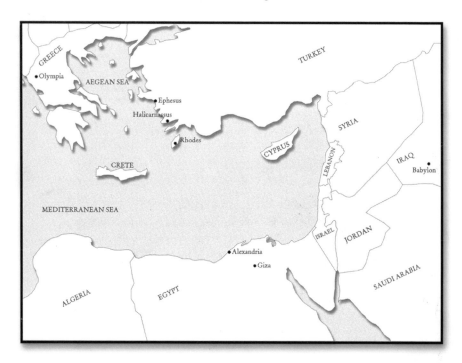

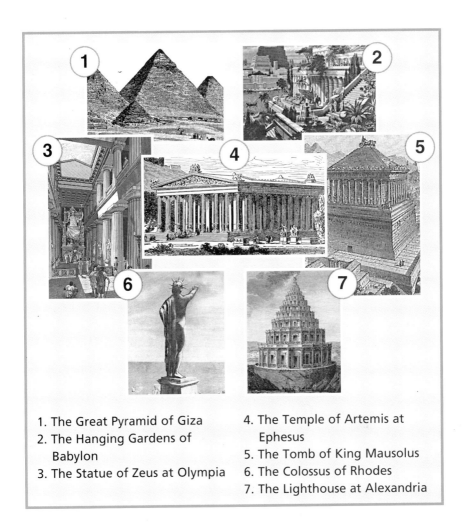

1. The Great Pyramid of Giza
2. The Hanging Gardens of Babylon
3. The Statue of Zeus at Olympia
4. The Temple of Artemis at Ephesus
5. The Tomb of King Mausolus
6. The Colossus of Rhodes
7. The Lighthouse at Alexandria

Many poets and **scribes** made lists of their favorite spots. These served as types of travel guides. In about 130 B.C., Antipater made his own list of favorites. He chose the number seven, a number the Greeks considered to be magic.

Antipater's list, the Seven Wonders of the Ancient World, is the one that has come down through history to modern times.

CHAPTER 2

The Great Pyramid of Giza

Rising 482 feet on the west bank of the Nile River, the Great Pyramid is the oldest of the Seven Wonders of the Ancient World. It is also the only one still standing today.

Like all Egyptian pyramids, the Great Pyramid at Giza was built as a tomb. The king, or **pharaoh**, who ordered it built around 2550 B.C. was Khnumu-Khufu.

King Khufu is often called by the Greek name Cheops.

The people of ancient Egypt thought of their pharaoh as the all-powerful sun god, Re. And, just like a god, Khufu was a strict ruler who demanded that everyone obey him.

All Egyptians believed a man or woman who died would have a life after death. For someone as important as a pharaoh, this new life must be lived among riches. And the pharaoh's body must be preserved so that the spirit could live on.

Thus the body of an important Egyptian was **mummified**. It was carefully dried and preserved with spices and salt. Then it was wrapped in strips of fine linen— 20 layers in all.

A pharaoh's body was buried with all the possessions he might need in his next life. Everyone wanted the pharaoh to be happy. His tomb had to be strong and tightly sealed. The mummified body and its possessions had to be protected from thieves.

Before the time of Khufu, important people were buried in holes in the ground. Above each hole, a low, rectangular tomb called a *mastaba* was built.

Step Pyramid

Early mastabas were made of mud brick. The roof might be either flat or rounded. The mastaba of a rich Egyptian could have as many as 30 rooms, placed in a long, low row.

In 2630 B.C., the pharaoh Djoser built an unusual tomb. It had started as a mastaba, but Djoser ordered it made of stone blocks instead of mud bricks.

He also changed the shape. His mastaba would not be low to the ground. When it was finished, Djoser's tomb looked like a giant staircase. It became known as the Step Pyramid. Pharaohs who came later liked what Djoser had done.

In 2550 B.C., Khufu became pharaoh. He declared himself to be the mightiest pharaoh ever. To plan for his death, he would need the greatest tomb ever built. He wanted it high up on the Giza Plateau. And he wanted a pyramid shape, not a long, low mastaba.

Khufu's tomb was to be very tall—taller than any building ever built at that time. Khufu's tomb was the height of a 50-story building.

The very finest stone was to be used—some of it from the Giza Plateau, the rest brought from **quarries** up and down the banks of the Nile. Such a pyramid would require two million huge stone blocks. And each of those would weigh at least two tons.

The work began. Although Khufu died after only 21 years as pharaoh, the work went on. In all, constructing the Great Pyramid took almost 30 years.

Let's meet Emron, the 14-year-old son of a pyramid worker.

Emron is excited. July has come, and harvesttime is over. The whole family has worked hard to finish picking and cutting the grains.

Each year, the Nile River floods their farmland from July to October. Farmers, like Emron's father, cannot plant new crops during this time. The river, spreading across their land, makes the soil too wet.

During the past two summers, Emron's father has left home in July to work on the pharaoh's huge tomb at Giza. Until this year, Emron was too young to go along. He stayed home with his mother and sister.

Now that he is 14, Emron is going to Giza to work on the Great Pyramid too.

"You will have to work hard," his father says. "The **overseer** will not let you come back next summer unless you do a good job."

When they arrive at Giza, Emron's eyes grow wide. The Great Pyramid is going to be huge! It measures 755 feet along each of its sides. The work has gone on for ten years. But the pyramid is only half finished.

Workers crowd the plateau at Giza. Soon there will be 50,000 of them for the summer work. There seem to be so many jobs to do.

Emron waits while his father finds a man he has worked with before. Emron's father is trained as a goldsmith. He melts gold and forms it into statues, belts, and jewelry. The man in charge of the craftsmen is happy to have a worker who is already trained.

Ancient civilizations did not use inches, feet, or meters. They used relationships to parts of the body when they needed measurements. The cubit was the basic unit of measure. These are some of the common measurements.

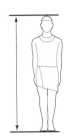

Average height = 4 cubits

Cubit = 1 unit

Foot = $\frac{2}{3}$ unit

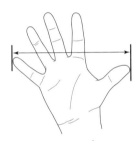

Great span = $\frac{1}{2}$ unit

Little span = $\frac{1}{3}$ unit

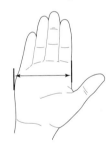

Long palm = $\frac{1}{6}$ unit

Short palm = $\frac{1}{7}$ unit

Digit = $\frac{1}{24}$ unit

Emron wishes he could be chosen for this important work too. But he knows he will probably be lifting and pushing huge stone blocks. Those are the jobs for young men who have no training.

The overseer looks at Emron. He thinks for a while. "You seem to have the slim hands of a craftsman," he says. "I will give you a chance to show what you can do. We have enough gold workers, but I need another toolmaker."

Emron is excited. He learns that many of the tools the workmen use to cut stone are made of copper. Others are of a very hard stone called *dolerite*. Men can pound a dolerite tool right through **granite** or **limestone**.

The handles of all the tools are carved from wood. Emron will first learn to sharpen tools. Then he will make handles for them. When he knows how to make these repairs, he will be taught to make new tools.

For shelter, Emron and his father build a small hut of clay bricks. It has only one room, but it is enough for the two of them. They will need it for only a few months.

When there are no tools to mend, Emron walks around the Giza Plateau. He stands and watches as hundreds of men work on Khufu's pyramid.

The men are in gangs, 25 men to a gang. A foreman calls out orders. The men move huge blocks of limestone, using strong ropes and **levers** made from heavy timber. Working together, they push and pull. Then they struggle to load each block onto a wooden sled and tie it down. Their strong backs bend under the hot Egyptian sun. Straining against the ropes, they pull at the heavy sled with its huge block. Slowly it inches upward onto an earthen ramp against the side of the pyramid.

Looking across the river, Emron sees other work gangs cutting into the hillside. They pull huge blocks of limestone to the water's edge. Tugging and straining, they load the blocks onto boats and sail them closer to Giza.

12

Sometimes Emron watches the stonecutters and the **surveyors**. He sees how men mix a **mortar** of sand, lime, and a great deal of water. When they spread the thin mixture on a limestone block, they can slide another block on top of it. Before the mortar dries, the men make sure the block is in just the right spot.

In a shady place on the plateau, some men draw on sheets of papyrus. This is a paper made from reeds that grow along the Nile. One day when Emron comes near, one of them tells him about the drawings. They are plans for a smaller pyramid Khufu has ordered. This one is for his wife, the queen.

Much about pyramid building puzzles Emron. He has many questions for his father.

One evening Emron asks, "How did the men find such a large, level site to build on?"

"I was not working here when this land was leveled," answers his father. "But my father was. He told me how it was done. The workers dug many rows of connecting trenches over the entire area where the pyramid would go. Then they filled the trenches with water."

"I think I understand," says Emron. "The top of the water would reach the same level in each trench, wouldn't it?"

"That's right," his father answers. "Workers marked the waterline on the sides of the trenches. Then they drained them. All the spaces between the trenches were cut down to the height of the marks. Later, the trenches themselves were filled with stone."

"So all of that was done before work began on the pyramid's sides?" Emron asks.

"Yes. And the pharaoh's outer coffin, the **sarcophagus**, was put in place so the pyramid could rise around it. When the pharaoh dies, a wooden coffin, with his mummy inside, will be brought into the pyramid through a long tunnel. This coffin will fit into the sarcophagus."

Emron is proud to be working on the pyramid. And he likes his job as a toolmaker. Now he knows how to make hammers, chisels, saws, and drills. As the summer passes, his work becomes more and more skilled.

One day, as October comes to a close, Emron's father hurries into their hut. "I have exciting news," he says. "When we go home in a few days, we will plant our last crop for a long time."

"How can that be?" asks Emron. "We are farmers. We need our crops."

"No," answers his father. "Now we are craftsmen. We have been chosen to come back next spring and work on the pyramid all year. Our whole family will live here."

"Can we build a bigger and better house?" asks Emron.

"Of course," his father answers. "We will have a house worthy of the pharaoh's best workers—for that is what we are."

What Happened to the Great Pyramid?

If you go to Giza in Egypt, you can visit the Great Pyramid of Khufu. But it will not be standing alone as it did in Emron's time. Khufu's son and grandson both had huge pyramids built next to it. There are rows of pyramids and tombs honoring Khufu's queens and relatives. There is also a **mortuary** temple where mummies were prepared.

When Khufu's pyramid was finished, a gleaming white limestone layer was placed over everything. It made the pyramid the largest and most beautiful building in the world.

But this outer layer of limestone is not there today. It was stripped off centuries ago to be used on buildings in the Egyptian capital city of Cairo.

CHAPTER 3

The Hanging Gardens of Babylon

In the 6th century B.C., there was an old and proud city in a land that is now part of Iraq. Called Babylon, it was the greatest city the ancient world had ever known. And it was the capital of a country called Babylonia.

Many kings had ruled Babylonia. Some were weak and did not defend their capital city well. Desert tribes often attacked and raided Babylonia. Some of these early conquerors were the Amorites, who ruled the area as a group of loosely connected **city-states**.

Then for 400 years, the conquering army of the Kassites occupied Babylonia. They governed wisely and established schools. Their scribes wrote myths and composed hymns to the gods.

But at last, the Kassites were defeated by another army, the Elamites. The Elamites **plundered** Babylonia and carried off many of the most treasured works of art. Then in later years, the fierce Assyrians overcame the Elamites and took over the land.

In 615 B.C., a brave man named Nabopolassar led the Babylonians into battle against the Assyrians and drove them away. The finest general in this struggle was Nabopolassar's own son, Nebuchadnezzar II.

When they fought the Assyrians, the Babylonians were helped by another tribe, the Medes. After the war ended, Nabopolassar and the king of the Medes, Cyaxares II, formed an **alliance**. If another war began, they would help each other. To seal their agreement, the two kings arranged that Cyaxares's daughter, Amyitis, would marry Nabopolassar's son, Nebuchadnezzar.

In 605 B.C., Nabopolassar died and Nebuchadnezzar II was crowned king. A strong military leader, he sent his warriors into surrounding lands to conquer other city-states. Thus his kingdom continued to grow.

Nebuchadnezzar wanted Babylon to be the finest city in the world. His workmen built huge buildings from clay. Each was decorated with sculpted figures of lions, bulls, and dragons. Where temples had begun to crumble, he **restored** them.

Nebuchadnezzar longed for Amyitis to be proud of their city. He hoped she would always be happy to be queen of Babylonia.

He built two walls around Babylon, one inside the other. Each was 50 feet high, and they were made of unbaked bricks. This double wall stretched for 14 miles on each side to protect the city from attack.

On top of the walls were large towers where men could stand. From there, archers could shoot a rain of arrows down upon anyone who might attack.

Babylon became a center for culture and learning for all of western Asia. Educated men from every part of the ancient world gathered there. Painting, sculpture, and music thrived.

The capital at Babylon was as beautiful as riches could make it. Nebuchadnezzar and Amyitis ruled from a royal palace that was the most magnificent residence in the world. Temples and **processional** walkways filled the city. Religious activities were conducted daily. The city contained 100 shrines to the Babylonian gods Marduk and Ishtar.

Nebuchadnezzar was proud of his city. But he still worried about his wife, Amyitis. He could tell she was homesick. Her people, the Medes, lived on a high plateau east of Babylon. There the air was cooler, and streams gushed with water. Trees and blossoming bushes grew everywhere—taller and greener than anything in Babylonia.

His capital at Babylon, though filled with beautiful buildings, was built on flat land. It stretched along both sides of the Euphrates River, which ran through the city. Farmers grew crops outside the city walls. But inside the city, there was no land for gardens.

The king thought of a plan. He would make his beautiful city even more elegant. And he would please Amyitis too.

19

Nebuchadnezzar set about designing gardens. They were to be set high into the walls of his largest palace. There they would be seen from all over the city. Even people entering the city would see them over the wall.

These Hanging Gardens of Babylon were 100 feet long by 100 feet wide. They were built up in terraces, like the seats in a theater or sports arena.

Nebuchadnezzar had huge stone arches, or vaults, built under the terraces and attached to the largest buildings of his palace. The vaults carried the weight of the planted gardens and raised the plants up to reach the sunshine.

The highest vault rose 75 feet in the air. This put it above the level of the tallest city walls.

Workmen filled each terrace with topsoil, deep enough so trees could take root. Beneath the trees, gardeners placed flowering bushes and plants. Some plants came to Babylon on river barges. Others filled carts drawn by oxen. These were Amyitis's favorites from the land of the Medes.

For months, workmen built and planted. Meanwhile, others dug a huge well into the lowest floor of the palace. It had three **shafts**. A special **irrigation** system allowed water from the Euphrates River to be raised from these shafts to the highest point in the gardens. Continuously, slaves on the lowest level filled leather buckets with water. Then others raised the chain of buckets. In this way, water reached even the highest gardens.

If you had visited Babylon in the days of Nebuchadnezzar and Amyitis, what would you have seen? Let's join Adzar, a young visitor to the city.

Every week, Adzar's father loads the back of his camel. He has gathered carpets and fine cloths from cities near and far. Now he will sell his **wares** in the crowded marketplace in Babylon.

Adzar is 14 now—old enough to go along. He walks beside his father's camel, eager to enter the mighty city. For him, the towering walls hold a world of surprises.

As they approach Babylon, Adzar and his father come to a stone bridge. It crosses a moat filled with water.

"This moat protects Babylon from attack," Adzar's father says. "At night, the planks of the bridge can be removed. Then no army can cross."

Adzar looks up at the huge **bronze** gate in front of them. This morning it is open. His father and the other merchants are welcome to enter.

21

"This gate is just one of eight that lead into the city," Adzar's father tells him. "Later, I will show you the blue and yellow Ishtar gate, dedicated to our mighty goddess of war. And you will like the Processional Way where important parades are held."

Adzar's father hurries to the marketplace and begins to set out his wares. Like much of the busy life of Babylon, the marketplace is on the banks of the Euphrates River.

Adzar begs his father, "Please, sir, may I explore the city streets?"

"You may go a short distance, my son," his father says. "I have brought seeds for the palace gardener. You may deliver them to him. They are for rare plants not seen in Babylon before. Soon they will be part of the hanging gardens."

Adzar goes through the streets as his father has told him. Along the way, he sees newer buildings made of baked bricks. They are more handsome than the sun-dried bricks used in earlier buildings, for some of those are falling into ruin.

Adzar marvels at the polished cedar beams used in the roofs of new buildings. Shiny tiles decorate the walls. Here and there, the buildings are trimmed with gold and silver.

In the center of the city, Adzar stares up at the seven-story temple-tower called the Etemenankia, or "House of the Platform Between Heaven and Earth." In the form of a **ziggurat**, it looms over the nearby temple to Marduk, the chief god of Babylon.

This city is a wonder, thinks Adzar.

Most historians believe the ziggurat to be the famous Tower of Babel described in the Bible.

But most amazing are the towering almond and walnut trees and bushes that hang from the palace of King Nebuchadnezzar and Queen Amyitis.

How green and cool they look! How bright the flowering
vines are that trail from the terraces. Figs and pomegranates
dangle over the walls. Though he cannot see them, Adzar
knows that foxes, rabbits, and small lions the size of dogs
live among the plants of the Hanging Gardens.

Adzar wishes he could live in such a palace and walk in the cool, green gardens.

As he comes near the palace, a guard hurries forward to question him. Adzar explains that his father has sent seeds. The guard calls for the chief gardener, who thanks Adzar and takes the package. Everyone seems interested in the new seeds.

Returning to the marketplace, Adzar finds his father talking to one of the scribes. These educated men record business transactions as they happen in the marketplace. Everyone respects the scribes, for it is important to keep accounts in order.

Adzar makes a decision. He will be a merchant like his father. And he will also learn to read and write. Then he can be sure his own accounts are in order when he comes to sell his wares in the wonderful city of Babylon.

What Happened to the Hanging Gardens?

King Nebuchadnezzar II died in 562 B.C. He was followed on the throne by a series of less-respected kings. They were not good military leaders. And many of them could not make good decisions. Babylon fell into decline.

What happened to Amyitis is not known. Nor do we know how well the gardens were preserved. It may be that the trees, bushes, and flowers were allowed to wither and die.

In 539 B.C., Cyrus, a Persian of the royal line, led an army against Babylon. His men poured through the city, destroying whatever stood in their way. Without any strong leaders, the citizens of Babylon gave little defense.

It is at this point that the Hanging Gardens of Babylon disappear from written records. Some historians believe that during the final struggle, the Persians set them ablaze.

Ruins of the foundations
of the Hanging Gardens

If you visit this part of Iraq today, you can see mounds of clay where the ancient buildings of Babylon stood. Men and women continually work to identify the buildings and streets. Some of the buildings have been restored.

Archaeologists have located the ziggurat, the Ishtar Gate, and the foundation of the royal palace. In the palace basement is a well with three shafts. Many historians are convinced these shafts held irrigation water for the Hanging Gardens of Babylon.

CHAPTER 4

The Temple of Artemis at Ephesus

When Antipater of Sidon wrote down his seven wonders, he drew special attention to one of them, referring to it as "the sacred house of Artemis that towers to the clouds." For Antipater, the beauty of this temple far exceeded the other wonders of the world.

Called by many historians the most beautiful structure on Earth, the temple was built to honor the Greek goddess of hunting, nature, and childbirth.

> The Roman name for Artemis was Diana.

The temple occupied the center of the ancient city of Ephesus, in what was known as Ionia. This land is now part of Turkey.

For the people of Ephesus, the worship of Artemis began in 800 B.C. The first temple built there was modest in size. So also was a second one built on the same spot. It was the third building that was the most beautiful and became the famous wonder of the ancient world.

This glorious third temple was built about 550 B.C. A Greek named Chersiphron was both its architect and its **engineer**.

Built in the Greek manner, the structure had 127 **marble** columns, each 60 feet high. The style of these columns was Ionic. That is, the height of each column was eight times the diameter at its base.

Many of these columns were gifts from neighboring monarchs. They were decorated with life-size figures showing the history of Ephesus. Among the columns stood dozens of bronze statues made by the most skilled artists in the land.

The temple was 425 feet long—about the same as one and one-half soccer fields. It was 225 feet wide. A central **sanctuary** held the statue of the goddess. It was a simple figure made of black stone, decorated with gold and silver.

Around the sanctuary were columns, two deep—14 pairs along each side, and 6 pairs along each end. Other columns formed a central passageway leading to the statue of the standing goddess.

Artemis was loved by all of Ephesus. And she was often honored by the people of the city with special celebrations.

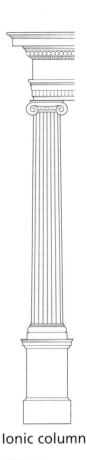

Ionic column

Let's meet 13-year-old Leana, a young Ionian girl, who has come to visit Ephesus and honor the goddess Artemis.

The waters of the Selinus River lap against the side of her family's boat as Leana steps ashore. A strong wind from the sea has blown the clouds away. Now Leana can look up toward the city, sitting on higher ground than the harbor.

There it is, she thinks. The wealthiest city in the world!

Crowds of people press around her. Here at the waterfront, hundreds are arriving by boat, in oxcarts, and on foot. But Leana hardly notices the crowd. She can only stare upward toward the wonder of Ephesus.

The city is just as her parents said. And rising above the rest of the buildings is the glorious temple. Its fine white marble glistens in the sun.

The great temple has been built to stand on an outside base with ten steps. Leana's father told her that a whole quarry of marble was needed below the ground to form so strong a base.

Leana turns to her mother and father. They're gathering the servants and the family's possessions.

"You were right," Leana says to them in a whisper. "This temple is truly the most beautiful building in the world! It's hard to believe I'm here at last."

"It was time to bring you," says her mother. "It was time you came to your first important celebration to the goddess Artemis."

Looking back up toward the temple, Leana can just make out the life-size, standing figure of a young woman— Artemis. It stands in a central window, looking down upon a **sacrificial altar**. Next to the altar is a columned building with stalls for 20 oxen.

Near the altar is a huge slaughterhouse. Here, all the city's meat is butchered under the eyes of the goddess. A great deal of meat will be needed for this year's celebration.

Leana's father leaves the harbor with some business leaders. She feels her mother's touch on her arm.

"Tomorrow, my daughter," her mother says. "Tomorrow you will see how the whole city turns out for the parade. It's the reason we have come to Ephesus at this time. Tomorrow is the birthday of the goddess, the sixth of Thargelion."

"Please, Mother," begs Leana. "May I go closer to see the goddess now? I want to see her golden lips."

"The time is growing late," her mother answers. "It will soon be dark, and we must hurry to the home of my brother. Tomorrow you will see wonders you will never forget."

29

The next morning, Leana is up before the sky grows light. The whole city seems to be stirring.

Leana looks outside her uncle's house. The sky is a clear blue. What a fine day it is for a celebration. As crowds form along the street, Leana hurries to dress.

For such an important day, the people of Ephesus wear their best clothes. These are dyed violet, purple, and crimson. The cloth for such fine robes is closely woven to make it strong.

Leana's gown is violet. All over it, gold beads dangle. Each is attached with a short purple cord.

The parade begins. First come the city's most important citizens, dressed in their finest clothes and jewelry. After them parade the priests and priestesses.

Then dozens of young citizens carry gold and silver statues high above the heads of the crowd. Each of these precious idols weighs more than three pounds. They have been kept in the **vestibule** of the great temple where they can be seen all year by visitors.

As Leana rises on her tiptoes to see the last of the statues, she hears the sound of a lute, a stringed instrument with a large pear-shaped body. Leana wishes she could learn to pluck the strings of such a fine instrument.

As the strains of the lute fade away, bronze horns and a chorus of drums send their music through the air. Behind the musicians comes a huge choir, the voices blending on the morning air.

Now it's time for the most important moment in the parade. The figure of Artemis Ephesia, the veiled goddess with **gilded** lips, is lifted high and carried through the streets. Boys and girls twirl and dance around her. Above it all rises the thick smoke of **incense**.

When the procession has passed all through the city, it winds back to the temple, where the figure of Artemis is returned to its position.

"Is it all over?" Leana asks.

"The parade is over," answers her mother, "but now everyone will celebrate with a feast of barley, bread, and **sweetmeats**. And for those who wish it, there will be wine."

"This has been a special day for me," says Leana. "I can hardly wait to come back next year on the sixth of Thargelion."

What Happened to the Temple at Ephesus?

Throughout history, the Temple of Artemis met with many tragedies. In 356 B.C., a man named Herostratus wanted to be famous. So he set fire to the temple. Even though the columns were marble, the tile-covered roof had been braced with heavy wooden beams. Once afire, these burned quickly. No one could stop the hot flame.

Twenty years later, when Alexander the Great conquered all of Asia Minor, he directed that the temple be rebuilt. When it was finished, he ordered it filled with fine paintings and other works of art.

Damage from earthquakes followed in 262 A.D. That same year, the temple was all but destroyed by Gothic invaders.

In the 4th century A.D., when most of the Ephesians had become Christians, the goddess was removed from the damaged temple and a cross was erected in her place.

There is no longer a harbor where Ephesus stood. Over the centuries, the changing water levels of the Selinus River caused layers of silt to cover everything nearby. When archaeologists searched for the Temple of Artemis in the 1800s A.D., they were forced to dig down through 15 feet of dirt.

Today, a broad field is all that is left of the Temple of Artemis and its altar. From this field rises a single column. It was erected by archaeologists to show, in a small way, the artistic style that marked this wonder of the ancient world.

CHAPTER 5

The Statue of Zeus at Olympia

You have read how the Temple of Artemis at Ephesus was famous for its great size and beauty. But the figure of the goddess there, though worshiped by all the Ephesians, was no larger than a human woman in size.

Another wonder of the ancient world was a Statue of Zeus, the king of the gods. This figure was huge—the height of a three-story building.

Zeus sat inside an open temple that was not much larger than the statue itself. An ancient historian wrote this about the artist.

> He has shown Zeus seated, but with the head almost touching the ceiling, so that we have the impression that if Zeus moved to stand up he would unroof the temple.

Zeus and his temple were located on the west coast of what is now modern Greece. The spot was called Olympia. It was an important religious center.

As the name Olympia reminds us, this was the site of the Olympic Games, first played in 776 B.C. The games took place every fourth summer at full moon. For a week, the best athletes of Greece competed in games of racing, jumping, throwing, wrestling, and boxing.

Although the Olympic Games had always been held to honor the mighty Zeus, at first there was no temple. It was not until around 450 B.C. that an architect named Libon was hired to build one. He designed a simple building with columns of the Doric style. That is, the height of the columns was six times the diameter at the bottom.

There were no good building materials in the area. So Libon made the temple of local rock, a porous limestone dotted with seashells. To make it more attractive, he had a hard white plaster painted over the limestone.

After a short time, the people of Olympia were not satisfied with this temple. Shouldn't it be more beautiful? Shouldn't it house a statue of the mighty Zeus?

In 435 B.C., they called for Phidias, the most famous **sculptor** of his day. Could he build them a statue to Zeus? It must be of the finest materials. And it should be surrounded by handsome **friezes**. This statue to the king of the gods would reign over all that went on at Olympia.

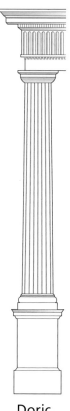

Doric column

The rules for the Olympic Games of ancient Greece were very different from those today. The only athletes permitted to compete were young men, and each of those had to be from a Greek town and speak the Greek language. Men who spoke a foreign language were called *barbarians*. Barbarians could watch, but not compete.

Slaves and women were not allowed anywhere near the games. To break this rule meant death.

Phidias began work on the statue. First, he and his helpers put up a wooden framework. This acted as a skeleton for the figure of Zeus. Then they carefully covered the framework with ivory and gold—ivory for Zeus's skin and sheets of gold for his clothing.

The ivory from the tusks of many elephants had cost a great deal. So had the gold. But now the people of Olympia had a god they could be proud of.

The Greeks thought of Zeus as both fatherly and very strong. He was a warrior who hurled thunderbolts. Thus his statue was shown as middle-aged. And it showed a muscular upper body. Over one solid shoulder was draped a golden cloak.

The throne of the seated god was **inlaid** with **ebony** and precious stones. Four figures in the shape of dancing women decorated the foot of the throne. Dozens of painted images of animals, gods, and sphinxes told of legends from Greek history.

The floor in front of the statue was paved in black stone. Around this stone paving ran a border of marble. The border encircled a pool of oil, which barred visitors from approaching the statue too closely.

In its time, it was the greatest statue in the world. Its period of glory lasted 700 years.

Let's meet Cronis and Boris, two teenage boys chosen to represent their city in the Olympic Games.

Groups of young men hurry along the dusty road toward Olympia. They travel in groups of two, three, and four. Cronis and Boris are proud to be among them. They have been chosen by the citizens of their town. Now they will be Olympic athletes.

Ancient Olympic footrace

The Olympic Games will not begin until a year has passed—a year when all athletes must remain in the city. All of them have trained from boyhood. Now they must use the year ahead for further practice in running, wrestling, and throwing the discus.

Each athlete prepares himself under the watchful eyes of special judges. Each will swear an **oath** to Father Zeus. And when practice begins, each will struggle against the others as if it were a matter of life or death.

Cronis is interested in the running events. Boris likes best to compete in wrestling.

As the two young men come close to Olympia, they see the Altis. This wall surrounds both the famous temple of Zeus and a smaller temple to his wife Hera. Nearby they can see the famous stadium, its grassy slopes waiting to seat 20,000 spectators. In the surrounding area, they make out places for throwing competitions and chariot races.

Boris stops to look at the scene before them. "This is what the men from the last Olympiad told us about. How honored we are to be here to compete in front of Zeus!"

Cronis nods. "If only we can make our families and neighbors proud."

Olympia is a shrine, but no permanent town is located there. So a marketplace has been set up for the use of the new athletes and those who would coach them. Everyone will sleep in tents or in the open air.

"I see a place for our tent," Cronis tells his friend. "It is a small spot, so perhaps we should claim it quickly."

"You are probably right," answers Boris. "But then let's hurry to the shrine. I want to gaze upon Father Zeus before the ceremony when we pledge our loyalty."

With their tent in place, the two hurry past Zeus's open altar, a mound of blue-gray ash and bone. For days, offerings have been burning there. Spirals of smoke still rise to the sky.

As they approach the shining temple, Cronis and Boris stop. At the doorway in front of them stretches the pool of oil. Cronis falls to his knees.

"Look how the setting sun shines off the oil," he whispers. "And how it reflects onto the face of Father Zeus. I have heard that the oil keeps the ivory from drying out and cracking."

Boris kneels beside his friend. "See how the golden cloak of Zeus shines too," he says. "Can you see the glass lilies that decorate it?"

When the shadows grow long, Cronis and Boris make their way back to the hillside camp. Tomorrow will begin a year of preparation they will never forget.

What Happened to the Statue and Temple of Zeus?

By 391 A.D., the Romans were leaders of the Christian world. The god Zeus was no longer worshiped in most of the lands of the Mediterranean. Because the Olympic Games honored Zeus, the Romans decided they should be ended.

The emperor Constantine ordered that the gold be stripped from all the ancient temples dedicated to pagan gods. He ordered the Statue of Zeus moved to his capital city, Constantinople. In 462 A.D., the palace containing the statue was destroyed by a fire that burned one half of the city. With its 700-year-old wooden framework, the figure of Zeus burned quickly. No trace of it was left.

During the 5th century A.D., a series of earthquakes shook the area around Olympia. What was left of the temple, its columns, and walls, were destroyed. Landslides followed. They filled the stadium where so many athletes had given their best.

Zeus and his temple were no more.

CHAPTER 6

The Tomb of King Mausolus

Mausolus was king of Caria, a city-state in the Persian Empire. His palace was in the capital city, Halicarnassus, in what is now southwest Turkey. This was less than 100 miles from the temple of Zeus.

Mausolus's father had been king of Caria before his son. When he died in 377 B.C., Mausolus inherited the throne. The young king was tall, strong, and handsome. A fine military leader, he was powerful in war. And he was a wise leader for his people.

Under the leadership of Mausolus, people of different races and from different regions worked together in the kingdom. Some brought Greek culture and architecture to Halicarnassus. Others brought the skills of the marketplace.

Still others saw to the raising of food for the population. Together, this multicultural population made the kingdom of Caria strong.

Mausolus married his sister, Artemisia. Even though such marriages are shocking to us, they were common in ancient kingdoms. When a city-state's king and queen were both from the same family, there was less chance of a takeover by enemies.

As King Mausolus became more and more powerful, he wished to be free of the Persian rulers. He had always preferred everything Greek—such things as art, music, writings, and fine food. So he declared Caria an independent kingdom and surrounded Halicarnassus with high walls and huge gates to keep back attackers. An inner fortress protected the city's spring, its source of drinking water.

Near the marketplace, Mausolus had two great harbors built, one behind the other. Warships waited at anchor there, another protection for Caria. On a spit of land across the bay he built a palace so rich and famous that it amazed the architects of that time.

For centuries, the people of the ancient world had buried their dead outside their city gates. Only rarely was a local hero buried at the city's center. Mausolus wanted to be buried as a hero might be, right in the middle of Halicarnassus.

He wanted a tomb for himself and his wife—one that would remind the world of his power and wealth. So the king built two main city roads. He pointed out the spot where they crossed. That spot would become the place for his tomb.

Mausolus called for the finest architects, sculptors, and builders to come to Halicarnassus. As work on the tomb progressed, he kept these craftsmen in his service for many years.

First came the base of the monument. It was 157 feet long and 63 feet wide—about one-half the size of a football field. Deep within this base was the burial room. It held space for two golden caskets. After Mausolus and Artemisia died, these would hold their ashes. The burial room was guarded by a row of larger-than-life stone lions.

As work progressed, the **alabaster** tomb looked more and more like a Greek temple. It was a beautifully columned rectangle with a pyramid-shaped roof. Almost 14 stories tall, it could be seen from all directions and for a great distance.

Battle of the Amazons from the Mausoleum of Halicarnassus

On one level were 36 decorated marble columns, and among those stood sculpted figures, each larger than life. Gods, horses, and Greek heroes were **depicted**. Additional statues decorated other levels of the monument. In all, famous sculptors created more than 100 figures.

The statue of a chariot drawn by four horses decorated the very top of the monument. Most historians believe that the man and woman shown driving the chariot were meant to depict Mausolus and Artemisia.

Mausolus died suddenly in 353 B.C., after only 16 years as king. His grieving widow directed the completion of the monument. It was finished three years later.

As Mausolus had wished, his ashes and those of his queen were **entombed** at the base of their monument, one of the Seven Wonders of the Ancient World.

And King Mausolus left something behind for us too— a word. It is from his name that we have come to call a large burial monument a *mausoleum*.

About the time of King Mausolus, powerful rulers began hiring *hagiographers*. These were special scribes who wrote about the gods and the powerful men who built temples and monuments to honor them. King Mausolus did not employ a hagiographer. He also did not hire artists to paint his picture. For these reasons, we know less about him than we do about other powerful men of his time.

What Happened to the Mausoleum?

The Tomb of Mausolus and Artemisia stood for many centuries. Then, about 1250 A.D., a huge earthquake struck the area. The topmost sculptures of the mausoleum crashed down upon the lower ones, knocking them off their bases. There the pieces lay—figures of gods, men and women, chariots, and snarling lions.

In the early 1500s, a Christian group called the Knights of St. John explored the ruins. They removed some broken pieces of the mausoleum and used them to build a castle nearby. Pieces of walls and chunks of sculpture were chopped up to fit the needs at the new castle.

Four hundred years passed. Then in the 1900s, both Danish and British archaeologists led expeditions to explore the site.

Today, portions of the marble statue from the top of the monument can be seen at the British Museum in London. But no sign of the Tomb of King Mausolus remains at Halicarnassus.

CHAPTER 7

The Colossus of Rhodes

The island of Rhodes was an important trade center in the Mediterranean Sea. On the island were three of the many city-states of ancient Greece. In 408 B.C., these three cities joined to form one government. They built their capital city on the island's best harbor. And they called that capital Rhodes, the same name as the island.

The soil on Rhodes was rich and fertile. The people of the island were contented and well fed. Fruits of all kinds grew there, and there were extra crops for trading. Sponges grew in the waters around the rocky coast. And these also were sold to merchants from other lands.

The people of Rhodes were clever traders, and the commerce of the island grew and grew. But as the island became wealthier, some other Greek city-states wanted to conquer Rhodes.

Pharaoh Ptolemy of Egypt was a friend. Many trading ships sailed between Egypt and Rhodes. So there was no threat of war from the Egyptians.

Grapes and citrus fruit were among the crops grown in Rhodes.

Demetrius

Among those who did want to steal the riches of Rhodes was a man called Demetrius, who ruled the Antagonids of Macedonia. In 305 B.C., Demetrius led his men in an attack against the island. For almost a full year, the people of Rhodes struggled to protect themselves against the invaders.

Rhodes was surrounded by a high, strong wall. Demetrius and his 40,000 men used huge siege towers and catapults against this wall. The outnumbered men of Rhodes grew weary of fighting. They lost many men in battle. But they would not give up.

Siege towers were tall, wooden structures built to be as tall as a city's walls. When they were moved up close, attackers could scale the outer wall.

Catapults were often part of a siege tower. These were like huge slingshots and were used to hurl rocks, arrows, and spears against an enemy.

Just as the Antagonids were about to break into the city, Ptolemy sent a fleet of ships from Egypt. They arrived just in time to help the defenders of Rhodes.

Demetrius saw the might of Egypt. Knowing he would be defeated, he quickly drew back. In their hurry to escape the island, the Antagonids left huge pieces of war equipment behind.

The citizens of Rhodes celebrated their freedom. How happy they were to have peace after so many months of attack. They gave praise to their sun god, Helios, for guiding them.

The island's leaders decided to build a great statue to Helios. And what better could they use for materials than the war machines left behind by Demetrius!

Soon they had melted down the bronze from all the war machines. It was molded to make the outer skin of Helios. The inner structure was an iron framework.

The statue was 110 feet high, more than 20 times the size of a man. And it stood on a white marble pedestal that rose another 50 feet in the air. A figure this large earned the title **Colossus**.

An architect named Chares of Lindos was chosen to direct the building of the Colossus. He was known for his fine work on statues. And he was respected as a soldier, too, for he had fought in the struggle against the Antagonids.

Chares designed the Colossus in the Greek manner. Although no ancient pictures exist, early historians wrote that the figure wore no clothing, but carried a cloak in his left hand.

With his right hand, Helios shielded his eyes as he looked out to sea. On his head he wore a spiked crown. It symbolized his role as the sun god.

Work began at the base. When the pedestal was finished, the statue's feet were placed on top. They were filled with heavy rocks to keep them steady.

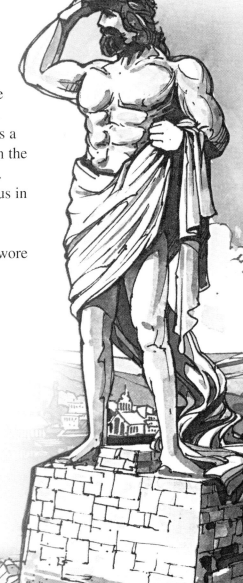

Working from the bottom up, the statue's builders gave the figure a firm framework—blocks of stone, bound together with iron. In fact, the famous writer, Pliny, says that the statue's core required as much work as did its final skin. Over this core were spread molded bronze plates, melted down from the war machines.

As the figure grew in height, the workers built earth ramps against its side. These provided footing for those installing the shaped bronze plates.

The ramps grew higher and higher. At last, the spiked crown on the head of Helios was completed. The ramps were removed. And the bronze was half-polished to give it the appearance of skin.

The exact spot at which the Colossus stood is not clear in the writings of historians. For many years, people thought the figure had stood at the harbor, with one foot on each side of the entrance. Calculations in later years showed that this pose would require the statue to be far taller than its 110 feet.

Other historians agree that the Colossus did not stand across the harbor's entrance. They point out that building such a massive figure at that location would have meant closing the harbor. Since the Colossus required 12 years for completion, it is not likely that Rhodes could remain a center of trade with its busy port closed.

What Happened to the Colossus of Rhodes?

The statue to Helios stood at Rhodes for only about 67 years. In 226 B.C., a strong earthquake shook the area. The Colossus snapped off at the knees. Broken parts lay all about the harbor. There they remained for almost 900 years.

Imagine that it's 44 B.C. The mighty Roman Empire has conquered most of the lands around the Mediterranean Sea. A man named Marcus has been sent from Rome to govern the island of Rhodes. With his assistant, Palus, he sails into the harbor and sees the huge pieces of the Colossus strewn about.

"There it is, Palus," Marcus says. "The famous figure of the Greek god Helios. Its broken parts have been lying here for nearly 200 years."

"I would like to have seen it in one piece," says Palus. "Did no one try to rebuild such a magnificent structure?"

"There was a time when it could have been rebuilt," Marcus says as he steps from their boat. "When Ptolemy was pharaoh of Egypt, he offered to have it put back together. But the citizens of Rhodes refused."

"Why would they do that?" Palus wondered.

"Their leaders went to an **oracle**," Marcus answered. "That wise man told them the statue had been destroyed because Helios was not pleased with it. The leaders of Rhodes believed what the oracle said. They decided not to rebuild."

The two men approach the ruins. Other visitors are beginning to arrive. Their costumes show that they are from many nations.

"Every year, hundreds come to see these ruins," says Marcus. He stops by a large section of the statue's shoulder. It would be possible for crowds of people to fit inside the cavity.

"Until we came here, I could not imagine the size of these parts," says Palus. "See how large the hands must have been. Each finger is the size of a large man."

"And this thumb," adds Marcus. He stretches his arms and wraps them around the broken thumb. His fingers do not quite touch.

As Marcus and Palus continue their exploration of the Rhodes harbor, they are convinced that they have indeed seen a wonder of the ancient world.

The End of the Colossus

In 654 A.D., a prince from Syria attacked and conquered Rhodes. He ordered the broken Colossus torn apart. Then he shipped the remains back to Syria on the backs of 900 camels. The bronze was sold, probably to make coins.

Nothing of the Colossus remains, but scuba divers continue to explore the waters around the harbor of Rhodes in hopes of finding a piece.

Today we have a reminder of the Colossus of Rhodes in our own country. When the French sculptor Frederic Auguste Bartholdi designed the Statue of Liberty as a gift from France to the United States in 1884, he is believed to have used the Colossus of Rhodes as his model.

CHAPTER 8

The Lighthouse at Alexandria

In the 4th century B.C. lived one of the most remarkable men in all history. His name was Alexander the Great.

Alexander the Great

Alexander was the first world conqueror. He led his armies throughout the entire world that had been civilized at that time. His conquests stretched from Greece to India and included all of the lands around the Mediterranean Sea.

Alexander chose Babylon as his capital city. From there, he governed his vast empire. To each conquered civilization, he brought Greek ideas, customs, and laws.

As his armies moved into other lands, Alexander founded new cities in Persia, Afghanistan, and Egypt and on the Mediterranean islands. Proud of his power as a leader, he named each of these cities after himself. By the time he died in 323 B.C., he had established 17 cities, each of them named Alexandria!

The largest and most important of these was a port on the north coast of Egypt. Alexander chose its location where the Nile River empties into the Mediterranean Sea. He founded this Alexandria in 332 B.C. when he was 22 years old.

The city quickly grew into a prosperous trade city for the Mediterranean lands. But Alexander was too busy conquering new lands to spend much time there. He turned the management of Alexandria over to one of his trusted generals, Ptolemy I.

Ptolemy made Alexandria into the center of the ancient world for science and literature. He built botanical gardens, an observatory to study the stars, and a medical school where students learned to **dissect** bodies. Hundreds flocked to the city. They came to study and meet with other men of knowledge.

Ptolemy also founded a magnificent library with the largest collection of books in the world. All ships entering Alexandria's harbor were forced to surrender any books they carried that were not already in the city library. The volumes were labeled "from the ships."

But there was a problem for ships that approached Alexandria's harbor.

Sailors in those days had no magnetic compasses to guide them. Captains had no charts of the waters they sailed. And lookouts had no magnifying eyeglasses. And of course, radar and sonar would not be known for 2000 years.

As ships approached a harbor, the sailors on deck and in the vessel's **rigging** peered through rain and fog to make out the shoreline. Did they spot a familiar hill? Was there a building rising above the land? Could they recognize rugged cliffs marking the entrance to a harbor? A man who sailed the seas in those days needed a great deal of experience.

The land of Egypt was completely flat. There were no hills or cliffs. And the **delta** of the Nile was so soft that buildings could only be built far back from the waters of the

Mediterranean. Thus a port was hard to find on the flat coastline.

In addition, the currents were strong and the surf was savage. Winds blew with a fury and often changed direction. If a ship came too close to shore while approaching Egypt, disaster might follow. Angry waves would pick the ship up and dash it upon the land.

Shipwrecks of this kind were common along the coast of Egypt. And the most dangerous spot was a low island off the coast of Alexandria. The island was called Pharos.

Ptolemy knew something had to be done to save the trading ships. Perhaps a tower that could be seen for many miles? He called upon wise men who knew the way of the sea. What could be done to stop the shipwrecks?

At that time in history, no one had ever built a lighthouse. It may be that such an idea was offered to Ptolemy. Or his advisors may have simply suggested a tower on the island of Pharos that could be seen by the crew of approaching ships. The idea of a light at the tower's top may have come later.

What we do know about the Lighthouse at Pharos has come to us through the writings of historians and from pictures on ancient coins.

An architect and builder named Sostratus was chosen.

The lighthouse took 20 years to complete. Built of white marble, it stood more than 400 feet high and had three sections, one on top of the other.

The whole thing rested on a square base. This contained a walled platform that protected the structure from the sea. Now that workmen were on Pharos, an **aqueduct** was built to supply drinking water.

The lowest level of the lighthouse itself was four-sided. It rose for nearly 200 feet and contained dozens of rooms for the staff. Each room had an outward-facing window to allow for a careful watch of the sea.

The middle section of the lighthouse was shaped as an octagon, and may have been 180 feet tall or more. It, too, had dozens of outward-facing windows.

The center of both these levels contained a sloping, spiral ramp. Up this ramp passed a continuous line of donkey carts loaded with fuel for the signal fire. The numerous windows of the tower lit their way.

The top story of the lighthouse was probably shaped as a **cylinder**. This structure held the light—a **pillar** of fire. An enormous **concave** mirror reflected the light out to sea.

Crowning the three levels stood a statue. Historians have long disagreed about which god it portrayed. Many have said it was Helios, god of the sun. Others argue it was Zeus, the protector. Still others insist the figure was of Poseidon, the Greek god of the sea. Other figures, less important gods, decorated the sides of the tower.

Near the lighthouse was a small, separate temple to the Egyptian goddess Isis. She was shown as a striding woman,

leaning forward as if to grasp and steady the masts of boats as they sailed into and out of the windy harbor.

Because Pharos was an island, a **causeway** was built to link it to the city of Alexandria. This was the route that brought workers to the island during the 20 years required to finish the lighthouse.

This causeway was also the path for the continual line of donkey carts bringing fuel. Some historians have said that the light was fueled by a wood fire. Others point out that Egypt had almost no trees to supply wood. They believe the light in the tower ran on oil.

> Over time, the Lighthouse at Alexandria came to be called "Pharos" after the island upon which it stood.

Ptolemy I died before the lighthouse was finished. His son, Ptolemy II, saw to its completion in 280 B.C.

Let's see how the lighthouse might have served trading ships from the north. Arno and Theo are seamen on a merchant vessel from the island of Rhodes.

Arno and Theo are on duty. They pace the deck, searching for any dangers their ship may encounter from the sea. Along 500 miles of Africa's coastline, they have seen no familiar landmark.

"I sailed through these waters last year," says Arno. "And I almost didn't live to tell about it."

"I heard about a ship that was almost driven onto the shore. They say no one on board saw the breakers rolling toward the land until it was almost too late," says Theo. "Were you in that crew?"

"Yes," answered Arno. "We couldn't see anything through the dark and fog. We were just lucky our captain thought fast and changed direction."

"This is my first trip to Alexandria," says Theo. "I hope we can spot the tower with the light on top. I hear it has saved hundreds of lives."

When the ship is still 35 miles from shore, a shout comes from the lookout in the rigging. Arno and Theo turn. They can hardly believe what they see from the deck.

"It's there! I see a light!" says Theo. "Just as we were told. Look, as that cloud of fog moves away, you can see it again."

"We should be in port tomorrow," says Arno. "And as soon as we off-load our cargo of fruits and sponges, we can load the hold again. The Egyptian cargo is always an interesting one. Besides ship's ropes and spices, we'll carry leopard skins and ivory from these lands."

"Now I can see why Alexandria is such a large, wealthy city," says Theo. "It has everything—people, money, and success."

What Happened to the Lighthouse at Alexandria?

Of all the seven wonders of the ancient world, the Pharos lighthouse was of the most benefit to man. It stood for 16 centuries, surviving a number of earthquakes.

In 1324 (some Egyptian records say 1375), a massive earthquake struck the lighthouse, destroying most of it. Later, a fortress was built upon the site.

Today, the lighthouse and the island of Pharos are gone. Alexandria has sunk into its harbors. Sand deposits washed into the Mediterranean by the Nile River have filled in the channel between the city and the island.

If you travel to Alexandria today, you can see the foundations of the lighthouse at Qait Bey Fort, built in the 15th century A.D. The fort is just one-fifth the height of the Pharos, the seventh wonder of the ancient world.

alabaster type of stone that is usually white and used for sculpture and decorative work

alliance association of two or more groups, individuals, or nations who agree to cooperate with one another to achieve a common goal

altar raised structure, typically a flat-topped rock or a table of wood or stone, where religious ceremonies are performed

aqueduct pipe or channel for moving water across a great distance

archaeologist scientist who studies ancient cultures through the examination of their buildings, graves, tools, and other things usually dug up from the ground

architect someone who designs buildings and advises on their construction

bronze hard yellowish-brown metal made from copper and tin that is often used to make statues

causeway raised path or road over a marsh or water or across land that is sometimes covered by water

city-state independent state consisting of a ruling city and its surrounding territory

colossus statue that is several times larger than life size

concave curved inward like the inner surface of a bowl or sphere

cylinder shape with straight sides and circular ends of equal size

delta triangular deposit of sand and soil at the mouth of a river or inlet

depict to show something in a picture, painting, or sculpture

dissect to cut and separate the parts of animal or plant specimens for scientific study

ebony blackish hard wood of an ebony tree

engineer person who uses science in the design, planning, construction, and maintenance of buildings or machines

entomb to put a corpse or remains into a chamber of a monument built to honor the person

frieze sculptured or richly ornamental band on a building

gilded having been overlaid with gold

granite coarse-grained rock made up of feldspar, mica, and quartz and used in building

incense substance, usually fragrant gum or wood, that gives off a pleasant smell when burned

inlaid set into the surface of wood or another material, usually to provide decoration

irrigation act of bringing a supply of water to a dry area, especially in order to help plants grow

lever
rigid bar that is used to  move or lift a load at one end by applying force to the other end

limestone rock formed from the skeletons and shells of marine life; used in construction

marble form of limestone that has been transformed through heat and pressure into a dense, variously colored, crystallized rock used in buildings, sculptures, and monuments

mortar mixture of sand, water, and cement or lime that becomes hard like stone and is used in building to join and hold bricks or stones together

mortuary relating to the room or building in which dead bodies are prepared and kept until burial

mummify to preserve the corpse of a person or animal for burial by embalming it and wrapping it in cloth

oath a formal pledge or promise

oracle someone considered to be a source of knowledge, wisdom, or prophecy

overseer someone who supervises workers, especially those engaged in manual labor

pharaoh ancient Egyptian title for a ruler

pillar something that is tall and slender

plunder to rob a place or the people living there or steal goods using violence and often causing damage, especially in wartime or during civil unrest

processional relating to a group of people moving forward in a line as part of celebration

quarry open excavation from which stone or other material is taken

restore to return something to an earlier and better condition

rigging ropes, wires, and pulleys that support the masts and control the sails of a boat

sacrificial relating to an offering to honor or please a god, especially of a ritually slaughtered animal or person

sanctuary most sacred part of a religious building

sarcophagus ancient stone or marble coffin, often decorated with sculpture and inscriptions

scale to climb up something, especially a steep incline

scribe someone who copies or writes out documents, especially in ancient times

sculptor artist who creates three-dimensional works of art, especially by carving, modeling, and casting

shaft vertical passage in a building

surveyor someone who takes accurate measurements of land areas

sweetmeat superior type of candy served at the end of a meal

tomb monument to a dead person, often built over the place where he or she is buried

vestibule small room or hall between an outer door and the main part of a building

wares things offered for sale

ziggurat ancient Mesopotamian pyramid-shaped tower with a square base, rising in stories of ever-decreasing size, with a terrace at each story and a temple at the very top

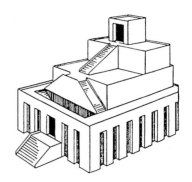

INDEX